D0428718

LIVE HANDS

A Key to Better Golf

BY E. M. PRAIN

WITH AN INTRODUCTION BY
BERNARD DARWIN
AND SIXTEEN PHOTOGRAPHS

WITH NEW NOTES BY
WALLY ARMSTRONG
&
TOM LEHMAN

SPORTSLOG
publishers

LIVE HANDS

SPORTSLOG
publishers

P.O. Box 9275
South Laguna, California 92677

Copyright © 1994
by Wally Armstrong and Tom Lehman

All rights reserved including the right of
reproductrion in whole or in part in any form.

Manufactured in the United States of America

First published in 1946 by A & C Black (Publishers)
Ltd., London, ENGLAND
Reprinted in U.S. and Canada by permission of Warde
Publishers, Inc.
Portola Valley, California

Library of Congress Catalog
Card Number: 94-69413

ISBN: 1-885198-02-7

CONTENTS

Illustrations

LIVE HANDS

PREFACE

This is no ordinary golf book!

Its uniqueness lies in that it was written by an extra-ordinary golfer. By that I mean the author was not a golf professional, yet he was a man intimately aquainted with the game.

Because of this he writes in a language that all golfers can understand. His writings reflect a passion and deep love for the game.

I've shared that same love all my life. I can't ever remember when the game hasn't played a major role in my life. From growing up in the cornfields of Indiana and being raised on the 9-hole Indian Lake C.C. course, which had one sand trap filled with dirt, to walking up to the 18th hole at Augusta, I have been blessed.

I have developed a great fascination for the game. I loved playing it, but preparing for the game was my passion. In college I had a passion for learning about golf and how to teach it.

While earning my Masters degree at the University of Florida, I had the privilege of working under the supervision of Conrad Rehling, one of the greatest teachers the game has ever produced. Conrad gave me a real heart for learning and teaching the game through the use of drills and training aids.

While I was on the Tour, I continued my studies into the game. I read thoroughly every golf magazine and book I could get my hands on. I tested my theories on my Pro-Am partners.

When I left the Tour in 1985, I began a full-time teaching career. As I studied the teaching styles of golf's great teachers, I began to appreciate the teaching of Earnest Jones, Percy Boomer, Peter Kostis, Jim Flick, and most of all, Davis Love, Jr. As Davis taught, he spoke a learner's language, using pictures, stories and feelings.

During the last 20 years of playing on the PGA Tour, teaching the game and conducting clinics all over the world, I have become more and more enamored with the historical golf books found in libraries and rare book dealers.

Every once in a while I would discover a real jewel of a book.

Live Hands is such a book. It is the most exciting book I've found, because it speaks to the very heart of every golfer.

The author talks about one central theme: the alliance of the clubhead to the hands to ignite the golf swing.

This is a key factor in teaching the game of golf. In all of my teaching I try to simplify the game and break it down into one simple swing thought as the foundation for my student's golf swing. Complexity should never substitute simplicity in golf.

I cannot agree more with the author in his description of how the average golfer gets tangled up with so many swing thoughts that it paralyzes him and prevents him from performing a fluid, effective golf swing.

LIVE HANDS

Every golfer of any level of golf will be able to identify with this book. It's author speaks in such wonderful, descriptive terms about his quest for the golf swing. He speaks of golfers as "life's most changeable disciples...always looking for Excalibur."

In his own quest, he simplified the game to it's very essence—that of simply swinging the golf club with your hands, with live hands.

Bobby Jones knew the value of "live hands." In his book, Bobby Jones on Golf, he says:

"We would all do better could we realize that the length of a drive depends not upon the brute force applied but upon the speed of the club head. It is a matter of velocity rather than of physical effort of the kind that bends crowbars and lifts heavy weights.

I like to think of a golf club as a weight attached to my hands by an imponderable medium, to which a string is a close approximation, and I like to feel that I am throwing it at the ball with much the same motion I should use in cracking a whip."

As I read the words of the author, I am drawn to his eloquent prose and his gifted ability to take the simple things in golf and make them profound. His writings remind me of the way Davis Love, Jr. taught.

It's my privilege to co-produce this book with one of golf's greatest Tour players, Tom Lehman. Tom has been a dear friend of mine for a number of years. If any one of his swing strengths stands out, it is his live hands.

Tom and I have the privilege of guiding you though this book with our footnotes, comments and insights from our PGA experience as Tour players, instructors and tournament champions.

We've tried to add enough comments to illuminate the author's original points while not too many to prevent you from enjoying the wonderful flow of the author's writing.

Also, I have included a few quotes from some old time teachers.

Live Hands

This is a book for all ages because the essence of the book deals with the heart of the golf swing.

I hope you will read this book again and again and that it will strengthen your game and give you an excitement and a love for the game that I have enjoyed throughout my life.

Wally Armstrong

PREFACE

I first met Wally in 1983 at the PGA Tour School at the TPC in Florida when I was a rookie and Wally was a Tour veteran. He took me under his wing and helped me successfully graduate. We became good friends and enjoyed time together outside golf with simple things like camping and fishing. And we've been friends ever since.

One day this summer, Wally called me up and said, "Tom, I've found this fantastic golf book first published in 1946. I'd like to re-publish it because I know today's golfer would really love it. Would you be interested in taking a look at it and giving me your comments?" Even though I don't read many instructional books, I said sure.

Once I read the book, my reaction was like Wally's. Everybody would benefit by reading this book. Plus it was fun to read.

Above all, I was impressed by Mr. Prain's insight into the mental side of golf. Mechanics play a big role in golf, but too much emphasis today is placed on analysis and mechanics. Many amateurs fall into the routine of focusing on technique and playing by the numbers; they try to follow steps one through 10 for a successful golf swing.

I have always played by feel on the PGA Tour. Mechanics are important, but feel brings it all together. This book reinforced my sense of feel in the golf swing.

While everyone may not agree on all of Mr. Prain's teachings of mechanics, everyone will agree with his focus on developing the feel of the golf swing. And, as he points out, the feel of the golf swing comes through the hands.

As you read this book, I hope that even if you don't agree with the mechanics described, that you recognize the value of his comments about developing the feel for the swing, and developing a strong mental approach to the game.

Mr. Prain reminds us that the object of the game is to get the ball from point A to point B in the fewest strokes and to do what it takes to get the ball in the hole.

I hope you enjoy reading this book as much as I did, and that it helps you get around the course in fewer strokes.

Tom Lehman

LIVE HANDS

INTRODUCTION

Mr. Eric Prain has asked me to be a curtain-raiser and I am very glad to do so, both because his book has interested me very much and because he is an old friend. I first met him when he came up to Cambridge as a freshman to join in the always laudable work of trying to beat Oxford. Later I have known him as one of a most famous team of Old Carthusians who constantly won the Halford Hewitt Cup at Deal and added to the gaiety of golfers in doing so. I have always thought of him not only as a very good player, but as one having a singularly easy, graceful and natural style. It comes as a complete surprise to read that he endured such agonies of theorizing before he settled down to the simplification of his creed. I can only say that no one would "know it on him." However, those past sufferings of his make all the more valuable his present confession of a simplified faith in which all such tiresome things as hips and shoulders and knees appear only as the followers—sometimes, as we all know, the very unruly followers—of the vital and dominant hands.

I must not steal Mr. Prain's thunder, but I cannot refrain from quoting one sentence of his which seems to be particularly commendable. Of the players in the Open Championship he writes, "It seemed that they had stayed behind the ball until after it was hit, and that the whole weight of the body flowed in behind the shot." That is well said. We have all felt at times that we could play so much better if only we had astral bodies that did not get in the way. He finds in concentration on the work of the hands a way of keeping those "too, too solid" bodies in subjection. This is the truth which he sings "To one clear harp in divers tones."

But though he sings it often, his song does not, if I may respectfully say so, grow monotonous; his tones are amusing as well as instructive. The best compliment I can pay him is to say that I am almost glad that owing to bodily infirmities, I can scarcely play golf any longer. If I could, so persuasive and exciting is he that I should certainly rush out onto the links and indulge in an orgy of practicing and come in several hours later, a physical wreck and having lost most of my few remaining golf balls. It may seem a double-edged compliment, but I mean it as a most sincere one, and with that I step aside and entrust the reader to Mr. Prain's entertaining hands.

Bernard Darwin

LIVE HANDS

I
SEARCHING FOR A FORMULA

As his ball sped into the bushes the length of a cricket pitch away following a disastrous shot with a no. 5, I heard a friend of mine mutter, "I cannot think why I play this beastly cold-blooded game." And then in the heat of the moment, he threw the offending club from him. As it flew through the air, straight up the fairway, and making in the direction of the green with an ominous swishing noise, his rage gave way to pleasure. "There," he said, pointing proudly as the club finished close to the flag, "I knew I had it in me: what length! what direction! what accuracy! and with just that suspicion of draw."

It is in moments of extreme indignity that we sometimes speak real truths. Of course, golf is not beastly, but it is a cold-blooded game and it gives us the time to think.

In other ball games, with the sole

exception of billiards, things happen so rapidly that we have to make up our minds and execute the stroke in that split second when the ball is coming towards us. There is no time for the intrusion of outside thoughts. Our mind tells us the stroke to play and our muscles obey the mind; the stroke has been played almost before we know it.

As time goes on, the heat generated by the body relaxes the muscles and we play more naturally than ever. Whether we are playing well or badly, our mind is fresh and our muscles have warmed to their work. We are not worrying how we do it, we are just getting on with the job.

As my angry friend said, golf is very cold-blooded. I have often wondered whether so

---

Wally: Arnold Haultain said it well: "In football and hockey you come to intimate and often forcible contact with the outer man. Chess is a clash of intellect. But in golf, character is laid bare to character."

In the hundreds of pro-ams I've played I've observed that most amatuers become trapped in indecision, frozen over the ball, thinking way too much. Plan your shot, step up and hit it.

much theory would have been written about it had it been a much faster game. Its very slowness leads to analysis and furthermore to self-analysis of a kind which is often muddling. The ball, if the truth be know, plays a brilliant defensive game. Confident in its own emplacement, it does nothing to interfere, but waits for the player to attack.

Consider the matter a moment in a mood of exaggeration. The course is empty and you are without a partner. You and the ball are about to start the intimate personal duel in which only one can survive. You know you must attack and you are wondering about your plan. The ball is perfectly calm and brilliantly on the defensive.

You tee up and grasp the club, perhaps a little quickly, and with a number of plans in your mind. You start the address, that preliminary reconnaissance, the probing of the enemy line. Then you launch the assault, trying to stick to one plan, but halfway up the backswing you decide that the time is not ripe.

You drop the club and light a cigarette, and you give the enemy a threatening look while trying to conceal your fear. You walk away and take in the surrounding view. Everything is very peaceful. Some cows are grazing quietly in the field to the right of the tee. A shot landing in that field will hardly disturb their peace, but you know that it will disturb you because it will cost you a stroke.

Trying to eradicate such thoughts you turn again to the tee, eagerly hoping that perhaps you can see a gap in the defenses. Everything is just as it was. The ball is impregnably calm, awaiting the expected attack. You walk to the start line once more, muttering as you go, "I wonder who it was

---

Wally: I love the way the author gives the ball a personality! I have experienced many times this battle in my own game. I like to tell my students, "Don't ever let the ball know you care so much!" "Be at ease, don't freeze." "Strut, don't stoop." "Glance, don't glare, at the ball."

Always focus on swinging the golf club rather than hitting the ball. We can't give him the advantage!

---

who said that this is a cold-blooded business."

Only good generals survive. They survive and are successful because experience has taught them the principles and techniques of their art. These principles are the basis of their plan, and when they have decided just how they will attack—or the shot they wish to play—they waste no time in attacking, confident of success because they are obeying those principles which have stood the test of time.

These are the good players, the players who know what they want to do and how they are going to do it. To the unpracticed eye, the methods they adopt may look somewhat dissimilar, but the good results

Wally: Only good generals survive. What a fantastic statement this is! And how true it is on the PGA Tour. Great players have developed their method, either consciously or subconsciously, to consistently play winning shots. They have an aura of confidence and determination that oozes from their approach and execution of the shots.

Develop your routine and believe in it.

they obtain are the direct outcome of an individual approach purposely based on old and accepted fundamentals.

The trouble with the rest of us is that we are always groping. We cannot grow as we should like because we have no roots. We are the earth's most changeable disciples, ever ready to try some new tag in the hope it will prove our salvation, equally ready to desert it for another if it does not give us what we want.

In my Cambridge days, besides playing a plethora of golf, I made a deep study of the theory of the game. I read most of the

Tom: I've always believed that golfers need to know their own game, what they're capable of and what they're not. Know these things so you can formulate a game plan and make good decisions for each course and each round.

Wally: This is a great description of the golfer who always finds himself grabbing onto a new technique or method. The swing doesn't have to be complex to be efficient.

Remember, start and finish a round with just one swing thought or image.

standard works, and I had, of course, ample opportunity to put these theories into practice. I do not think it an overstatement to say that I ran the whole gamut of theory.

I can still recall, in some degree, my mental attitude to the game at that time. I do not know how many times I felt I had found Excalibur. One day my salvation lay in the movement of my hip, the next in the way my shoulder turned, and again I felt I had found it when I opened my somewhat closed stance.

Looking back on it now I know I should have played better had I made the best of my obvious limitations. Instead of wallowing in a mass of theory I should have employed a merciless sifter. I should have been quicker to see how little was really important.

> *Tom: I'm a firm believer in finding what it is that you do well, and working to perfect it. For example, I draw the ball naturally, and I've spent 25 years working to perfect my draw, rather than spending the same years searching for how to hit it perfectly straight. The result is a shot that I can trust in all circumstances.*
> *Develop a consistent shot you can trust on the course.*

I found the meat in the end, but it took me too long to discard the fat and the stuffing. I make these personal observations only because I know the hopeless feeling which assails the changeable disciple. How fleeting are the moments of success and how often the new half-built castle tumbles about him in ruins!

After the spacious 'Varsity days I became a spasmodic week-end golfer. I played mainly with friends, many of whom were in the higher handicap grades. It was then I began to realize how large was the world of theorists and how great was their self-castigation.

I noticed that many of my friends arrived at the clubhouse intent upon enjoying their

Wally: Every golfer can identify with the search for new, easy fixes.

Only 8% of the golfers in America have had a lesson.

Find a good, qualified teacher and take a lesson to find solutions. Because there are no quick fixes and as teacher Bill Strausbaugh says, "Golf is learned, earned and acquired."

game; but as soon as the game had started, they played as if under a cloud. They were often rather worried and in some cases frustrated and miserable.

I soon discovered the reason. In the course of one swing they were trying to do six or seven different things. But all that they achieved was an exaggeration of certain actions of that swing which deprived the whole of rhythm. Their minds were focused on these motions instead of on the ball at their feet. They had forgotten the first principle in golf which is to hit the ball. Their play was unduly slow and they made a business of pleasure, while their game, far from improving, took a sharp turn for the worse.

As I have already said, around the apron strings of golf there hangs a mass of theory,

Tom: This is what I call paralysis by analysis. All that really matters in golf is the score on the scorecard. Golf is a game you should play like an art form; it should just flow from who you are. How it gets done is of no real importance as long as you can score.

some of it good in its way, but much of it very confusing. The more we think of this point or that, the more we vacillate. Somehow we must get down to the meat and discard the fat and the stuffing. It is true that for those who have the leisure and patience to do it, this separating process yields much available knowledge; since it is only by trial and error that we can learn for ourselves what is unessential, and then, with the courage of conviction, rebuild on what we know to be a sound and practical basis.

The week-end golfer, however, is hardly in this position. He has to earn his living, and he has neither the time nor the opportunity to make radical changes in his game. For radical changes cannot be made in the course of eighteen holes. If, in the course of a round, such changes are attempted, they lead at once

Wally: Famous teacher J.H. Taylor says, "I am certain there can be no freedom and no natural swing in hitting the golf ball if the mind is occupied by instructing the body." Think of the swing as one circular swing, not as many parts.

to a state of mental confusion the same as I notice in many of my friends, and to which I have referred before.

A successful change of style takes much time and hard work. It can only be accomplished over a period under the guidance of the local professional, or through frequent visits to some quiet corner of the course in the company of a bucket of balls. When playing a game——be it only a friendly one—the enjoyment is increased and the results are better if we concentrate on one thing only, namely to hit the ball.

Wally: Realize that habits begin as tiny cobwebs and through years of repetition become steel cables.

Develop a good, clear, simple picture of what changes you need to make and map out practice to make them.

But when you're out on the course trust your practiced feelings to deliver the ball to the desired target.

Tom: I can't think of a better example of this than Nick Faldo. Nick decided to rework his swing under the guidance of David Leadbetter. They had a clear goal in mind; it wasn't done just for their health. The result is that he is now one of the top players in the game today.

Live Hands

As in other things, so in golf: we must be content to make the best of what we have. We are either too old or too wicked, to relinquish the habits of years. We have formed our style and we have not the urge or the time to make extensive alterations in it. In using to the best advantage the mould we have already fashioned lies our best chance of enjoying the game and of achieving results in keeping with our merits.

What then are we to do with this unwieldy mass of theory? Clearly we must swallow it in a severely tabloid form. We must extract from it only the vitamins, leaving the bulk to others with more time and better digestion. A process of compression is required whereby all the by-products are eliminated until we are left in the end with the highly concentrated nourishment.

The object of the ensuing chapters is to show in some detail what, in my view, remains when this process of compression is complete, leaving only in the heated crucible the ingredients of a practical formula which can be applied in all circumstances.

It does not claim to be an easy and sure road to scratch, like the correspondence course I once saw advertised, which invited the reader to attain such a handicap by means of six simple lessons. Instead, it aims at improving the present results of the weekend golfer in the higher handicapped grades by an easily remembered means which can be applied to his game with the minimum of mental effort. Consciously applied at first it will soon become a habit.

I

THE GRIP AND THE STANCE

George Duncan, the player in this photograph, is about to start the back swing. Note the perfect overlapping grip. The hands fit the club as if they had been designed especially for it. They form two V's on the shaft, and those manipulative fingers, the forefinger and thumb of each hand, are squeezing the sides of the shaft, feeling for the clubhead. Already the hands have assumed control.

Note also the easy stance: the player gives an impression of relaxation. There is a total absence of tension. The knees are slightly flexed, and the feet are comfortably placed.

Tom: The best example to watch today of a tension free swing is Phil Mickelson. There isn't an uptight bone in his body. Remember to relax on the course.

LIVE HANDS

II
THE ALLIANCE OF HANDS
AND CLUBHEAD

If you were to ask a man with an unpracticed eye what impressed him most while watching an Open Championship, he would probably say that it was the ease with which the players executed each shot. The whole thing appeared so effortless and easy that it was annoying to admit that one could not play just as well oneself. No one motion or mannerism, common to them all, stood out so clearly that one could say with certainty that there lay the secret of good golf. All he could do would be to sum up the spectacle broadly, remarking that each swing had polish, a combination of control, balance and timing.

This broad observation would be true, but he would have missed the secret by which these players attain such outstanding ease. It would be correct to say that they did not all stand alike to the ball, that some swung flat and others upright, that some swings were short and others long, but the more practiced eye would notice one point common to them all.

Their hands controlled the club throughout, and they hit the ball with their hands.

The class player gives an impression which I can only describe as "live-handed." His hands are always doing something. They dominate the swing to such an extent that no other movement in it stands out for all to see. It is this factor which produces a spectacle of smooth and rhythmic ease. It is this factor, too, the control for the club by the hands and the hitting of the ball with the hands through the medium of the clubhead, which makes

Wally: I can't agree with the author more with his observation of the great players that he watched during his life.   As a young boy I can recall being caught up in the same observation.   Watch a championship in person or on TV today, and you'll see the same characteristics.

the first-class golfer. It is, in fact, the Excalibur which raises him out of the ruck. It is the secret of good golf, and of better golf by the week-end golfer.

The importance of the hands is not a discovery. It is as old as the game itself. In doctrines about the game, both written and verbal, it has often been mentioned before. But I think it has been content to lie modestly submerged, depressed by a lot of theory about hips, shoulders and pivots, there to be discovered by those who delved, but eluding the less persistent. It is time it came to the surface.

If we are honest with ourselves we know that, as week-end golfers, we are far too prone to make too much use of the body. We suffer, if you like, from too much body urge.

How often have we said—after a particularly disastrous shot—that we hit the ball with the stomach? This is not so much a metaphor as we should like to believe. The phrase carries this much truth, the body has

II
IMPACT PLUS

Walter Hagen's ball has just left the club. Notice the position of (a) the body, and (b) the hands. The body and shoulders have returned to their position at the address. The hands have traveled across the body curbing the strong desire it has to turn towards the hole.

got there first. It has got there first because we have failed to allow the hands to control the clubhead. In the course of the swing we have lost the feeling of that particular part of the club with which, after all, we were designed to hit the ball. With nothing left to hit with, at some point in the swing the body has decided to take control. With nothing to offer instead, and desiring to remove the ball from its present position by means either fair or foul, we permit the eager body to proceed with results which we know so well.

This struggle between the body and the hands never ceases in the average golfer. The pity is that the body invariably wins. I am sure that it wins only because we have not realized the importance of swinging the clubhead with the hands, and of making sure

---

Wally: It's so easy to get the cart before the horse. The body will naturally want to take control in hitting the ball with a forceful move. This takes the hands out of the shot and the swing is often destroyed. That's when the searching begins. Remember, control your swing with your hands and let your body follow.

that the hands hit the ball through the medium of the clubhead. If we are thinking golfers at all, we are so obsessed with some movement or other in the swing that we focus our concentration on it instead of devoting our mental energies to feeling and swinging the clubhead. The hands are dead; the body is too much alive.

As the hands are the only part of the player in direct contact with the club, it is only right and logical that they should be in control. They are invested with that sense of timing without which all is lost. We all know that in order to deliver a blow, the clubhead

Wally: The hands truly are the navigators in the golf swing. If you don't have a feeling for a good golf swing through the hands, then there can never be a consistent swinging of the golf club in the heat of the battle on the course. Make your hands your navigators.

Tom: Golf, more than anything, is a game of feel. When you watch Seve Ballesteros play, it is so easy to sense the feel and touch he has. This rhythm and feel begins in the hands. Try to develop this feel.

must describe an arc. Obviously it cannot do this of its own accord. It must be intimately connected with it. Clearly the hands are that influence. We must use them; they must navigate throughout.

If you are doubtful of the importance of the hands, try this experiment for yourself. Tee up a ball and standing with the feet together, hit it as hard as you can using the hands and wrists. You will find that the body turn is minimized by the fact that the feet are locked. There will, of course, be a slight turning of the shoulders and hips which will come to pass in a natural manner since, by reason of the locking of the feet, there is no other means of swinging the club except by

Wally: The author here describes the most common drill used through the centuries of golf instruction. It's a drill that all golfers should use every time they're on the practice tee.

Feeling the hands swing the clubhead in a circle around the body is the most important feeling any golfer can develop. The hips, the body, the legs, the shoulders—everything forms a support base for swinging the club with the hands in a circle.

the hands and wrists.

It is just such a feeling that we wish to engender. Avoid as far as possible any lifting of the body as you take the club back. If you really use the hands, this lifting will not take place. There will be a slight feeling of impotence, due to the shutting of the feet, but take your courage in both hands and hit the ball with them. I think you will be surprised at the distance and direction obtained.

"When you get married," it is often said, "begin as you mean to carry on." In golf this is sage advice. Get away to a good start and you greatly improve your chances of finishing in control. The hands must be given the chance to set the clubhead in motion.

But their purpose does not end there.

Wally: When teaching beginners I use a club where the bottom of the grip sticks directly into the face of a 5-iron. This lets them see that their hands truly are the clubface, and what they do with their hands will directly affect the face of the club throughout their swing.

Remember this union of the clubhead and the hands.

III

THE TOP OF THE BACKSWING

George Duncan is beautifully posed at the top of the backswing. Notice the hands. They are still firmly in control, knowing precisely the present position of the clubhead. Under the direction of the hands, the hips and shoulders have turned, and the full power of the body is concentrated ready to be applied as required by the hands.

Wally: It appears that Mr. Duncan has collapsed his swing, but really he has placed his hands in a beautiful position at the top to allow his arms to extend on the down swing.

Centrifugal force will stretch the arms straight, and pull them into a nice, powerful, extended position through the ball.

It's far better to have soft stretched arms and the correct hand position than to have a rigid left arm and a rigid swing.

They must retain that feeling of the clubhead throughout the stroke. The clubhead must be an animate thing living in the hands. It must not become supine or dead. This is the very feeling that subjugates the body, an offending bulk which, if it is not properly controlled, will interfere just when it is least required.

The trouble with most of us is that we put the cart before the horse. We look upon the golf swing as a series of movements made by various parts of the body whose sum total will eventually bring the clubhead to the ball, and the various antics which the body and feet perform are dictated by the hands in the journey they make through the arc of the golf swing. If the hands are in control, those movements we worry so much about are resolved in a natural manner.

Tom: Former University of Minnesota golf coach, Les Bolstad, taught me to see the whole picture. Even when working on only a certain part of the swing, always see it as part of the whole, starting with the pre-shot routine right on through to the flight of the ball, the spin on it and how it will bounce once it lands.

THE ALLIANCE OF HANDS

So far as the golf swing is concerned, in order to keep any part of it in perspective we must review the action as a whole. For it is at its best an unbroken motion. To stress one part unduly must destroy the rhythmic flow. There is a time and a place for each movement, and none should be consciously forced into place until the timing of the machine is ready to receive it. Each will fit in a natural manner when it is really required.

No venture can be successful unless someone is in control. It will not do if the various members dash here and there, accomplishing this and that on their own account without regard to the doings of others, uncertain if their efforts have a direct bearing on the object, not knowing if they are being duplicated in some other quarter. There must be a master unit which directs, plans and controls. The golf swing is a rhythmic motion, and every rhythmic motion has a guiding, controlling force.

When we swing a golf club, what exactly

is our object? Our object is to hit the ball with the clubhead, attaining at the same time the maximum speed and accuracy at the moment of impact. We cannot achieve our object unless we have some form of control. To function efficiently, that control must be vested in something with an intimate connection with the clubhead. The hands are the only part of the body in direct contact with the club. Clearly they must control.

The spectator at the Open Championship, in his broad summary of what he saw, remarked that control was a feature of all the players. They gave a decided impression of playing within themselves. It appeared that they had a carefully husbanded

---

Wally: Famous instructor, J.H. Taylor, talks about this connection, "The soul of golf is timing. The timing of any golf shot is felt in the motion of the clubhead, when the hands and fingers are in complete control, all through the stroke. As far as possible put your brain into your hands, let the ankles, knees and hips do their movement as subconsciously as possible, and let your thoughts live only in your hands—delicate, sensitive and obedient hands."

---

reserve ready to be used whenever it was wanted. This impression was created because, through the feel of it in their hands, they swung the clubhead and brought it to the ball with the maximum speed and accuracy at the moment of impact. It seemed that they had stayed behind the ball until after it was hit, and that the whole weight of the body flowed in behind the shot.

In other words, they hit the ball with the hands through the medium of the clubhead.

The movements of each players' body were perfectly synchronized. It was all so smooth that you could not detect one motion from another. This pleasing camouflage was achieved because all these movements were controlled. The whole performance looked natural because, through that intimate feeling between the hands and the clubhead, and not through any conscious thought on the parts of the player, these movements fitted easily into place.

They appeared functioned and faded

IV

THE RETURN JOURNEY

Gene Sarazen has begun the downswing. The hips and shoulders are unwinding and the hands are moving downward to a point where they will turn in towards the ball. Notice how the hands support the clubhead.

Wally: This is a classic position. Watch, study and feel it. Notice that just prior to impact, Mr. Sarazen is still flatfooted and his hands are moving into the ball; this is much like skipping a rock on a lake. This image is one I've given throughout many of my video tapes. When you look at the picture, don't try to analyze it, just feel that position.

without disturbing the rhythmic flow since they were not forced or studied. They remained natural since they could not do other than they did. Controlled by the hands they are natural movements and follow as night follows day. Really they are not our worry.

Some years ago in America I was discussing golf with Johnny Anderson, who was at that time Olympic discus champion. Johnny was a good golfer and a student of the game. He told me then that the function of the hand was no less important in discus throwing. He explained that when his body preceded his hand at the moment of the throw, the length and direction suffered. The discus flew off to the right and the throw was

> *Wally: I love this discus analogy. Often in my instruction I will have a student hold a Frisbee and make a motion around the front of his body like a discus thrower. The hands and arms swing in a circular manner in front of the player. A golf swing should feel the same way, a circular swish in front of your body with your hands. Look for that feeling.*

some feet short of normal. But if the hand came through first, pulling the weight of the body behind it, the throw was both long and straight.

The analogy to golf is exact. The hand in each case provides the motive force, directly in discus throwing and indirectly in golf through the medium of the clubhead. Hand control ensures that the full weight of the body is massed behind the shot and applied in its proper place.

Balance was mentioned as another quality common to all good players. How then do we achieve it ? If balance was not natural in everyone, they could not stand comfortably in a room nor could they walk down the street. The first is balance in a static condition; the second is balance in motion.

We are apt to think of balance as something to be consciously attained, perhaps by a studied transfer of weight from one direction or another. If left to its own devices balance will look after itself for it is a gift natural to everyone. It is born in us. The good golfer achieves it because he is content to let it function naturally. If all movements of the golf swing are synchronized by means of a supreme control, balance is bound to follow.

Sometimes I have heard the remark, "I shall never improve at this game. You see, I have no sense of timing." What then is timing? Applied to golf, one definition might be that timing is the co-ordination of mind and muscle which brings the clubhead to the ball with the maximum speed at the moment of impact. Yet the same people who doubt that this valuable sense is in them have no difficulty in knocking a nail into a piece of

Wally: I find in my teaching, if a player learns to swing the golf club in a circular manner around his body that balance will take care of itself. The key is to teach a person to swing the golf club first and to stay in control of the swing around the body. The body will simply make its adjustment to compensate for the swinging motion.

wood with a hammer. Perhaps they have not looked at it in this light, but such a task requires a sense of timing. If they can do this, anyone can, though some are more skilled than others, then the sense is there all right. It needs to be developed.

Compared to a golf club a hammer lacks balance. The golf club is a more sensitive instrument. The head of the hammer is heavily weighted and there is no mistaking its presence. But the golf club has a finer balance with the feel of the head less pronounced, and unless we are alive to its significance, we lose the most valuable adjunct in helping us to play well.

So much mental energy is wasted thinking about hips, shoulders, the left arm

Wally: In my teaching I've found there to be no greater way to improve timing than to work with the student in using simple drills to accentuate the swinging of the clubhead with the hands. Try this drill:

With your feet together, start with short beltline swings, then work to longer swings. Feel the timing in your swing. If you cannot make a short swing using your hands, how can you ever move out to a full swing?

V
HALF-WAY POINT
ON THE DOWN SWING

Arthur Havers is taken at the halfway point on the downswing. The hands are about to turn inwards and bring the clubhead to the ball. By virtue of their unquestioned control, the body is severely disciplined. The right side is beginning to move into the stroke, but its activities are governed by the alliance of the hands and clubhead.

Live Hands

or the right elbow, all of which will look after themselves provided they are controlled by that close relationship between the hands and the clubhead. The closer the relationship which exists between these two the better the sense of timing. Anyone can improve their timing, and *ipso facto* their golf by a studied effort to encourage this bond.

The other day I played a few holes with a member of the local club. I had not played with him before and I think his handicap was six. He had an ungainly style and an upright swing, and I was amazed how consistently he hit the ball down the middle of the fairway. The ball flew from the club with a sweet mellow crack.

Interested by results from methods so seemingly unpolished I watched carefully for

---

Wally: Jones said it nicely: "Golf is an art. And those who think of golf being a science have unfortunately tried to part from each other the arms, the head, the shoulder, the body, the hips and the legs. They make the golfer a worm cut into bits, with each part wiggling in every-which-way direction."

the reason. I found the answer in the hands. The shoulders and hips moved the bare minimum and the face of the club was shut throughout. It seemed at first that the result should have been a hook or a smothered shot. But the player's hands saved him. From start to finish of the swing they were firmly in control, swinging the clubhead and bringing it through to the ball.

I found that in the course of his work he used his hands a great deal. I believe his "live-handedness" was brought about by an unconscious effort on his part. They were strong, and it was natural for him to use them. I do not believe the player knew to what he owed his success.

It is a pity that as we grow older we lose that youthful gift, the faculty for imitation.

Wally: Today's average golfer is too into analyzing his swing rather than using his mind to create a good clear image of the golf swing and using that image successfully.

Use mental pictures and images of movements from other sports to create strong images for your game.

Live Hands

Young boys and girls who start the game early acquire a natural swing by watching and imitating some good player. Many have a fine swing without ever having a lesson. Many also can give a truly life-like imitation of the eccentric methods of players they have seen. If the youthful eye is quick to grasp the right way to swing, it has also an unerring capacity to reproduce something unusual.

I remember how proud I was as a boy of a reproduction I often gave of a player I once saw at St. Andrews. With the precociousness of youth, I used to delight in the amusement this imitation gave to grown-ups.

This man was standing on the sixth tee of the Eden Course. The hole runs parallel to the shore of the estuary of the River Eden. Since the fifth green is so close to the sixth tee, it is both a safety precaution and a matter of common courtesy not play to the green until the players in front are off the tee. Another small boy and I were patiently waiting to approach the green as we watched

The Alliance of Hands

this gentleman tee up.

He began with a series of ungainly and vicious waggles which increased in fury, if not in beauty, until he had made nearly fifty. At last his clubhead came to rest behind the ball. It would soon be over, we thought. But not at all. He remained there rigid and immobile, a fixture like the peaceful landscape in an effort, one assumed, to hypnotize the ball to yield to his will.

Nothing broke the silence save the lapping of the waves on the shore. I looked at my watch and I timed him. For a minute or more nothing happened. I had the urge to laugh. One felt that tense expectance which sometimes assails one when waiting for an explosion. Just when it was least expected, and as if a button had been pressed,

---

Tom: I see this all the time in Pro-Ams: amateurs freezing at the ball. Tension is the result of this lack of flow. And the result of tension is bad shots which translates to bad scores (unless you're the world's greatest putter and chipper). So remember to relax and let your swing flow.

VI
COMING INTO THE BALL

Walter Hagen has reached a later stage in the swing. Here the hands have begun to turn inwards to bring to clubhead to the ball.

everything happened at once. A mighty heave of the body synchronized with a wicked lunge.

The performance was over in a flash and his swing—if you can call it such—was the shortest I have ever seen. Needless to say he was playing by himself for no one could have stood that for a round. We passed through him soon afterward still searching for his ball on the beach. His performance, of course, was easy to imitate and I believe I could still do it now. Perhaps he was a hypnotist on holiday who had played much hockey in his youth.

One day shortly before the war I was playing golf with a friend at a well-known course where Mr. X was the equally well-known professional. Mr. X was a famous stylist. We had finished our round and we made our way towards the caddy-master's shed to pay off our caddies. While waiting for some change I happened to glance out of the window, and I saw in a rough patch of grass at the back of the shed a small boy swinging an old and rusty iron. That boy had a lovely swing. I collected my change and went straight out of the shed towards that patch of grass. The small boy continued time after time to swing the club with a beautiful ease.

"Who taught you to swing like that?" I said.

The boy looked up at me in surprise.

"No one taught me, guv'nor," he replied. "I done it like Mr. X."

The very young have the advantage in that they are not analytical. For them it is sufficient to swing the club, leaving the whys and wherefores to their poor misguided elders. This passion for analysis has been the downfall of many fine natural swingers. Not content just to swing the club they must find out how they swing it. They enter the labyrinth of theory, some of them never to

Wally: This is an incredible paragraph which shows how easily children can swing the golf club. Remember this the next time you watch a PGA Tournament on Sunday afternoon. You may improve your game.

emerge. It is a stage through which most good golfers pass. They forsake the naturalness of youth for the inquisitiveness of adolescence. If they survive, and most do, it is a valuable stage in their golfing education. It gives them experience. They emerge from that stage decided in their own mind what are the governing factors which go to make the golf swing. They are more sophisticated, more philosophical, less credulous than they were of the magic properties of pet theories. By trial and error they have found what matters in the golf swing, what makes it at its best a lovely, rhythmic motion.

It is we, the week-end golfers, who are the eternal gropers. We are the gullible public, ever ready to invest our surplus energy in any casual theory, basing all our hopes upon it, working it to death,

Tom: Harry Caddell, a long time Tour caddy reminds me, "Don't think, just execute", and "Turn off the brain and turn on the game." What he's saying is don't get in your own way by over-analyzing everything. Be more like a fearless kid, and like the Nike slogan says "Just do it."

exaggerating its importance, and finally discarding it in disgust when it proves to be just another South Sea Bubble. The hips, the shoulders, the elbows and the feet all have their part to play, but each must be controlled and allotted its place in the whole. That control lies in the hands whose henchman is the clubhead. The more these two are allied, the better the golf we play. Someone said of the perfect golf swing that it was the poetry of motion. Alas! How often ours is prose cut up into strips.

To keep our hands alive, we must be alive to our hands.

Wally: Realize the importance swing stability and confidence can have once practiced and trusted.

Remember, "To keep the hands alive we must be alive to the hands," is the very essence of the golf swing.

Tom: You can't generate clubhead speed without moving your weight properly and turning your shoulder and hips. You can't hit straight consistently by hitting only with your hands. You can't have good rhythm if you have lousy footwork and posture. Everything works together. The important thing to remember, then, is that the feel for it all comes through the hands.

VII

THE MOMENT OF IMPACT

Craig Wood taken at the moment of impact: the hands are still dictating. They are saying to the body "Stay where you are. We'll tell you when we want you." By reason of their mastery, the player's weight is coming in behind the shot. Although the clubhead is now traveling at maximum speed, its speed is still controlled. The body is balanced and ready, awaiting the word from the hands.

Live Hands

III
SOME AIDS TO LIVE-HANDEDNESS

By rights this chapter should describe in detail how to obtain this feeling of the clubhead in the hands. It might be expected to reduce the golf swing to sections and to show in each, what the hands are doing, why they do it, and what effect they have on other members of the body. But I should not be true to my creed if I deviated at this point into the paths of analytical theory. For the golf swing is not a meccano which can be pieced together by screws.

I stick to my theme that the secret of better golf is to swing the club with the hands and to hit the ball with the hands through the medium of the clubhead. Other actions of the body, subsidiary to this control, can be left to look after themselves. It is better to confine the attention to the alliance of the hands and the clubhead. For this combination pays dividends. Yet now I feel I am bound to suggest to the reader some aids for making him more live-handed, and to examine with him certain points in the swing where the hands are in danger of defeat by the body.

After a period without playing, the good golfer finds on restarting that his hands have become dead. Many have the feeling that their clubs are ounces lighter. The weight of the clubs has not altered, but this lighter feeling is brought about because the hands have lost tone. Lack of exercise has rendered the muscles duller and less sensitive. The clubs feel lighter because the hands cannot sense the clubhead. After a round or two this feeling begins to return, and the revival brings with it a marked improvement in results.

The more we swing the club, the more supple and sensitive the hand muscles

Wally: The golf swing is not a machine which can be pieced together by screws. The central theme of all my teaching is to build a picture of a circular swing. Feel that circular swing and then trust that circular swing when you go to the practice tee or golf course.

become, and the quicker that spark is generated from the clubhead to the hands. So the first thing we must do is to tone the hand muscles.

I am afraid my past is strewn with the wreckage of many carpets, and therefore I do not advise daily practice on the best Persian at home. A few swings each day in the garden or on an old mat are quite sufficient to tone the muscles. If this is impossible, select a club from your bag, grip it in the fingers and then waggle it a few times, striving with each waggle to feel the clubhead.

Some people take great pains. During the war, an airman friend of mine had little time for golf and yet he was quite determined to keep in touch with it somehow. So he used

Wally: I remember as a young caddy meeting touring pros Lionel and Jay Hebert. Every time I came by to deliver clubs to their room they had a golf club in their hands. As they talked they moved the club back and forth in the air. You could see it in their swing, they had a definite "live handedness." The club was welded to their hands and their hands were alive to the clubhead. Both Lionel and Jay won the PGA Championship.

VIII

THE MOMENT OF IMPACT

Henry Cotton, a great exponent of live hands in golf, is taken at the moment of impact. This position is a fine example of power perfectly controlled. The body is disciplined and the leg muscles are braced while the clubhead is traveling at tremendous speed under the guidance of the hands. How solid they look on the club!

to take up with him an ugly, weighted stick which he waggled secretly in his cockpit, no doubt for the sake of his muscles, and perhaps for auld lang syne!

The grips which golfers use are as varied as hibiscus in Ceylon. Many very good players have an unorthodox grip, and I have even seen a scratch player who gripped the club with his hands reversed. Yet although they may vary in type, they all obey one principle. They grip the club in the fingers.

The most important fingers in each hand are the forefinger and thumb. In an article the other day I saw these forefingers described as the "trigger" fingers. That is to say, in order to grip correctly, the forefingers are bent as if for pulling the triggers of two pistols, while the thumb rests lightly in each case against the top joint of the forefinger. In this manner the thumb and forefinger of each hand form a V on the shaft of the club. This combination of forefinger and thumb is really the feeler in each hand. As they pinch against the sides of the shaft, the presence of the clubhead should become more pronounced. These two fingers in each hand are the manipulative fingers. It is mainly through them that the clubhead is felt. They are the aids to better timing, the key to better golf.

No magic is wrought by the remaining fingers. They function naturally, gripping the club easily and avoiding any tightness or tension. Too tight a grip reduces the feeling in the fingers. Do not be afraid of gripping lightly. The club will not fly out of the hands at the moment of impact, for the natural reaction is to tighten the grip as the clubhead comes to the ball.

The overlapping grip has probably the most followers, and it is certainly the most common among the better players. Since the hands are joined by the overlap of the right little finger on the forefinger of the left, the overlapping grip has the advantage of helping

Tom: This is not to say that you put a choke hold on the club, but the message here is clear: feel the clubhead with your fingers.

to keep both hands moving in unison. It has come to be regarded as the standard grip in golf.

Having taken the correct grip, the next thing is the stance. It is at this point that so many players lapse into the grotesque. Stand at the first tee of any club on a weekend and you will be able to count on the fingers of one hand the number of players with a natural stance. It must be something psychological, the terror of meeting the ball, which causes so many contortions. The correct way to stand is the way which feels most natural to the player. It is often a matter of build. The taller player will probably have a wider stance. It is more natural for the splay-footed

Wally: The author's teaching on the grip is really sound—some of the soundest teaching I've ever read.

In my teaching I sometimes have people hold a toy pistol to show the position of the wrists. Then I simply transfer the aiming a pistol to holding the club.

Beware that you don't grip the club in your palms like a baseball bat. This will deaden the hands from producing their whip-like action through the ball, which is necessary for distance and accuracy.

to turn their feet outward; the reverse will apply to the pigeon-toed.

Tension in any form must be avoided, since tenseness at this early stage will remain for the rest of the swing. It is only a matter of placing the feet comfortably and of inclining the body from the trunk upwards slightly towards the ball. Do not reach out to the ball. Do not stoop. Be comfortable.

The knees should be slightly bent with the knee joints relaxed. This will help to give a smooth pivot on the back swing. The ball should lie on a line drawn from just inside

Tom: This is a part of my address position that can ruin everything that follows. I tend to slouch, or stoop, to the ball rather than keeping my spine straight and bending from the waist. This is especially true when I'm tired. This poor posture results in poor swings, swings where I've lost my feel for what I'm trying to do. Remind yourself to maintain good posture even when you get tired.

Wally: This again is great teaching advice. Remember that the setup merely places the body in a position for the hands to do their work —it allows the hands to make a consistant powerful orbit around the body.

IX

AFTER IMPACT

Bobby Locke taken just after the moment of impact; it is obvious from this photograph that the hands and clubhead have worked in unison. together they are following the ball, now on its way to the green. Note how the right side, when properly controlled, comes in easily behind the shot. All the spectators but one are looking to see what has happened. That one, a more discerning gentleman, is looking to see how it happened. Is he watching Locke's hands?

the left heel. Since the left hand is above the right on the club, the left shoulder will be uppermost with the right shoulder lower and nearer the ball.

So far we are gripping the club easily in the fingers and feeling the clubhead with those manipulative fingers, the thumb and forefinger of each hand. We are standing naturally, avoiding any tension. If there is no tension, and if we are gripping the club properly, we shall feel the clubhead as we waggle the club in the address. This is its main purpose. A spark has jumped across from the clubhead to the hands. In the address we are cementing the alliance between the clubhead and the hands. We must see to it that nothing comes between them for the remainder of the swing.

The first check point is the beginning of the back swing, and it is here that many

Tom: I totally agree with this. Building this bond, this feel, between the clubhead and the hands creates confidence to pull off the shot.

players go wrong. So often at this point you see the player raise his shoulders. This is brought about by picking up the club instead of swinging it. By raising the shoulders, the player has immediately changed the plane in which the arc of the swing should be described. In order to neutralize this, there must be a compensating movement, and it appears in the form of a drop of the shoulders on the downswing. There is a tendency at this stage to break the wrists or to take the club back with the left hand only, leaving the right hand to hang loose and lifeless on the shaft. It is true that the left hand must guide, but the right hand must work in unison with it. Therefore, feel for the clubhead with the manipulative fingers of the right hand.

We are going to use BOTH hands at the ball and so we start them back together. If you are PRACTICING this motion try to decapitate an imaginary daisy growing eighteen inches behind the ball. But if you are

LIVE HANDS

PLAYING a game, dismiss the daisy from your mind and think only of hitting the ball.

The beheading of the imaginary daisy will give the swing a broader arc, thus affording the hands and the clubhead more room to maneuver. The break in the wrists will come naturally. It is sufficient to say that these members will pivot over the ball. Do not worry about them, concentrate instead on feeling the clubhead in the hands and, with them guide it to the top of the swing.

The start of the downswing is the second check point. All will be well if the feeling of the clubhead is there, but if it is absent the body will begin to dictate. The result will be that the body will lead the hands and win the race to the ball. The body must be restrained,

Wally: For practice, stick a tee in the ground 10 to 12 inches behind the ball, slightly inside the target line, then brush your club across the tee on your backswing.

Tom: Davis Love III is a great example on tour today of someone with a big arc. Watching what he does and copying it can only help.

thus giving the hands and the clubhead the time and space they require for their task. Using the hands as a medium, bring the clubhead smartly through the ball. In other words, hit the ball with the hands.

What happens once the ball is hit does not really matter. It is on its way and nothing we may do can alter its course. But if the hands have really hit the ball, they will carry the clubhead through to what is popularly described as a "gallery" finish. This "gallery" finish is not a special performance enacted for the benefit of press photographers. It is the natural outcome of a swing in which the hands have played the predominant part. It is a feature of all good players, but it can be possessed by anyone who controls the

Tom: One of the most common faults among amateur players is that they start the downswing with their arms and shoulders. This causes them to get "over the top" or outside the proper arc of the swing. The feet and knees initiate the shifting of weight to the left side, in a smooth and rhythmic way to allow the hands to remain in control of the clubhead and in the proper hitting position.

X
AFTER IMPACT

A fine action picture of Ed Dudley; between this position and Locke's there is a difference of a fraction of a second. His clubhead, like Locke's, is following the ball and the hands are allowing the body to move in behind the shot.

LIVE HANDS

clubhead with the hands.

Watch the first-class professional before he plays each stroke. He selects his club and then stands a pace or two behind the ball, studying the shot he is about to play. All the time he is considering the stroke, his hands are moving and alive. They are flicking the club to and fro in a kind of miniature address. This is not a mannerism but an unconscious effort, the outcome of habit, to feel the clubhead in the hands. It is a brief rehearsal of the performance which is about to begin. The spark is jumping across from the clubhead to the hands.

I have often wondered if it would be

Wally: Swing to the finish, that's the key. Not at the ball but through it. In a good swing the ball simply gets in the way of the swing. Alex Morrison wrote in 1932, "Golf is not a matter of hitting the ball but of swinging a club. Hitting the ball is merely incidental to making a swing."

Tom: This is right on the money!! Feel the clubhead in your hands.

sounder to teach the beginner to play the short shots first. It is natural when we begin to crave for a full-blooded blow at the ball. The occasional one we hit stays in our memory for days. Most of us would lack the patience to continue if we were restricted during those agonizing initial stages to the bread and water of half-swings. We require a good portion of jam in order to keep our appetite. And yet if we were Spartan, I feel it would pay handsomely. Begin as you mean to carry on! And if we developed a solid beginning, the rest would seem more simple. From the standpoint of control it is easier to lengthen a swing than to reduce it, and it is ironic that in golf the nearer we approach to the hole the harder the game becomes.

For reasons too obvious to state, of all the shots in golf the short shots are the most telling. The steepest climb along the road to scratch lies between that mark and four handicap. These last few strokes are the most difficult of all to discard. As a rule, it is in the short shots that the solution lies. No one can become a good scratch golfer without an effective short game. Rhythm in this department is essential, even more necessary perhaps than in the longer shots. Yet the same principle applies: feel the clubhead and hit the ball crisply with the hands.

It stands to reason that the nearer we are to the hole the less body turn we require. So many handicap players pivot too much, as if relying on the turn of the body, and not on a

Wally: I work many hours with my students on short, mini-swings. I have them swing a club from beltline to beltline, keeping the club in front of them and through the impact area. It's the best way to train to feel the proper swinging of the club.

Wally: Most people don't practice enough from 60 yards and in. The fact is 60% of most golf scores come with short shots. But the discipline to practice short shots takes a commitment on a player's part.

Watch the Tour players practice and you'll see how much time they practice around the greens. You'll realize how important practicing in this area is. Practice your short game.

crisp hand action, to send the ball towards the hole. In the short game, more than ever, we must strive to be live-handed. We can afford from the half shots downward to restrict the body turn, to stay more over the ball, and to let the hands and clubhead do the rest.

And now a word of warning: the easy wristy pitch as played by many good golfers is a pleasantly artistic sight, but it requires a nicety of timing which only natural gifts and years of playing can bring. Such a delicate stroke is too ambitious to be copied by the week-end golfer. For those of us whose play is spasmodic, it is better to use in shots around the green, a little more forearm, a little less wrist. I do not mean by this that the shot should be stiffly played, but mix with a

---

Wally: I love the author's description of the pitch shot! There needs to be a mix of relaxed hand action with a pinch of solid forearm.

Swing the forearms in a nice, forceful pendulum, and allow the hands to simply ride along; feel the club face, and work the blade through the ball.

XI

THE "GALLERY" FINISH

Abe Mitchell has played a No. 5 iron shot to the green. How beautifully easy it seems! He might have just knocked the head off a daisy before playing the real shot. His hands are alive all right. Notice how their absolute control has given to this finish a look of delightful ease.

Wally: If a swing is made correctly, the arms and elbows should naturally drop to the sides as Mr. Mitchell demonstrates so beautifully. I love this picture. In addition to being a great player, Mr. Mitchell was also one of golf's greatest teachers.

buoyant hand action a pinch of solid forearm.

The short shots are best regarded simply as drives in miniature, and the same principle holds. Grip lightly; stand naturally; avoid tension; feel the clubhead in the hands, and mindful always of its purpose, swing it with them crisply through the ball.

Tom: A lack of tension is even more important on short shots than for long shots. Distance, control and touch can only be achieved with a fluid, tension-free swing.

IV
MAKING A PLAN

In an earlier chapter I suggested that the ball was brilliantly on the defensive and awaited with confidence the assault of the player. The time the player has for thought is the strong point of this defense. I suggested also that only good generals survive, and I firmly believe this is true. The plan of attack must be sound, based on solid, well-tried principles, and those advocated here are to swing the club with the hands and to hit the ball with them through the medium of the clubhead.

First we must think hard and constructively, and then we must act quickly while the plan is fresh in the mind. It is fatal

Tom: All that any sports psychologist can ever teach you is summed up right here. This is a goal: commitment. A golfer must survey the shot, make a plan, commit to it, and do it. Second-guessing is never part of the equation. Watch Tom Watson play and you'll see what I'm talking about.

to change the plan half-way through the operation. The result will then be confusion. It is equally disastrous to allow any thoughts of failure to cloud the shape of our object, and we shall not succeed if the mind is focused on something other than this object. The object, of course, is to hit the ball a certain length in a given direction.

It is not our object to turn the left hip, nor to keep the right elbow close to the side on the backswing since neither maneuver, though good in itself, can of its own accord make us hit the ball. Each is only a tactical move in the general plan. Prior to hitting the ball we must first have a clear-cut picture in our mind of the shot we are going to play, and we must retain this picture throughout the stroke.

Let us consider again the faster games. In lawn tennis we cannot decide the next shot we shall play until the ball is coming at us from the other side of the net. Lawn tennis differs from golf in that our opponent can directly influence our next stroke. As the ball comes over the net, we decide at once to play a forehand shot into our opponent's backhand corner. We have at most a couple of seconds in which to make up our mind and lay the stroke. Whether the ball pitches on the base line or in the cabbages at the back of the course is quite another matter. The fact is that there is little time in which to dwell on cabbages. The very short interval between the resolve and the completion of the stroke helps us to think constructively, since there is little time for indecision.

It is the same in cricket. The batsman has that very short period from the time the ball leaves the bowler's hand to the playing of the stroke in which to make up his mind. If we are facing someone like Larwood, the time is, indeed, very short. Our mind quickly tells us that the stroke required is a drive through the covers, or a glance to leg, and our muscles quickly set about going through the necessary motions.

XII

THE "GALLERY" FINISH

The perfect ending by Henry Cotton; this photograph illustrates how easy tremendous power can look if it is properly controlled. The hands have completed the arc of the swing and "the whole weight of the body has flowed in behind the shot."

LIVE HANDS

Although in golf our opponent cannot directly influence our stroke, many other things can. Although tennis players need not be cabbage-conscious, most golfers have been in their time acutely aware of woods. Sometimes it has seemed impossible to keep out of them. Bunkers have thrown out their magnetic fields and water has given them a wintry stare. The game of golf was not devised so that a time limit is set for the playing of each stroke. There is room for vacillation.

In order to counteract this, we must see in our mind the shot successfully played, even before we play it, and as I have already said we must retain this picture of perfection, to the exclusion of everything else,

---

Wally: Welcome trouble as friends. See the trees, bunkers or water at the side of the fairways as pointing you to the fairway. Envision them as directing you toward your target. Imagine the trees, the water hazards, the O.B. stakes, simply giving you definition to your target.

A great player will turn these problems into friends. And in golf, attitude is our greatest weapon.

throughout the swing. Having formed a clear picture of how the shot must be played, we must waste no time in playing it. Good bridge players maintain that if tricks must be lost, they should be lost quickly. Many of us find this easy whether we play fast or slow. And yet it is good advice. To play quickly has virtue. It suggests decisive thought. Furthermore, it helps to retain in our mind the unblurred picture of the successful shot.

As the ball disappears into a bunker, how often has one heard the remark, "Oh! I knew I should do that." This is an immediate admission that during the stroke the player was thinking of that bunker. He had not filled his mind with the positive picture of the ball carrying successfully over it. How then do we form this picture? Standing on the tee before driving we decide in our mind the point on

Wally: Most amateurs spend too much time thinking about the swing without a good image of their goal. They don't take enough time to visualize the shot before they play it. Remember what I tell my students: "he who hesitates is O.B."

the fairway at which we wish to play. We then form a picture of the ball flying through the air and landing on the selected spot. This picture we retain until the stroke has been laid. It is extraordinary how the muscles will obey the dictates of the mind.

Then again, we may be faced by a long second shot up to the flag with an awkward, unsympathetic wind blowing off the left shoulder. Our first thought is perhaps rather gloomy. We see our ball swinging away to the right and disappearing into deep rough far away from the green. It is better to try and replace such thoughts with the pictures of the shot held firmly into the wind, and with this fixed in our mind to set about hitting the ball.

It helps before playing a short pitch, or any stroke around the green, to select the exact spot where we wish the ball to land. Plan the complete shot. See it in the air, see it

Tom: Les Bolstad taught me not only to see the ball flying through the air, but to see the spin, see the way the ball bounces once it hits the ground, and see the direction it rolls as well. Try to visualize this each shot.

land on the selected spot with just enough run to take it to the hole.

To consider perfection before every stroke may seem to many a conceited and ridiculous practice. Why, they may ask themselves, are they receiving strokes from scratch if they are not among the sinners? It is true we shall fail wholly, or in part, to attain our ideal on many occasions, but we shall fare far worse without a plan which, if it does not unfold to perfection, may well provide us with a thoroughly workable solution. Moreover, the mind is giving the muscles something constructive on which they can set to work.

How many of us, I wonder, play for position? Nearly any two-shot hole has one or more ways in which it should be played.

Wally: Images are always more powerful than commands. The brain will react to what it sees, then will send signals to the muscles to carry out the picture.

Visualize your shot first. Then, trust images you see, and trust the mechanics that you've practiced and simply be a shot maker.

XIII

THE SHORT PITCH

A.L. Bently has played a short pitch to the flag. Short shots should be regarded as drives in miniature, and the same principle holds—control the clubhead with the hands. This principle is well illustrated here. The hands have brought the clubhead crisply through the ball, and together they are following it on its way towards the flag. Note the easy position of the body. No muscle is forced or strained.

The topography should be studied. From what place on the fairway, we should ask ourselves, do we get the best second shot? Most of us are content to drive straight down the middle without regard to the conformation of the ground and bunkers around the green. The golf architect, however, is more subtle than we suppose, and unless we study the lie of each hole, he will lure us away from the path of true righteousness. To aim from the tee with a driver at a few square yards of fairway may seem an ambitious project for us, the weekend golfers, and yet we are constantly aiming at a green, a target seldom much larger.

Greens, too, have their subtleties and the contours of many are so shaped that they suggest to the player either a hook or a slice. These are traps into which we shall surely fall unless we observe them and make such adjustments as are necessary in the playing of the shot.

Making A Plan

Some years before this recent war, that great golfer and showman, Walter Hagen, came to the last hole in the Open Championship at St. Annes needing a two to tie. The hole itself was over four hundred yards long. After a good drive down the fairway he was faced with a No. 3 iron shot which he knew he must hole.

He paused for a moment behind his ball studying the shot, and then when everyone expected him to select his club and play it, he started to walk forward to the green. Once at the green he made a detailed survey of its contours, deciding where his ball would pitch and how it would turn on to the hole.

Oblivious of the dense crowd and of the skeptics within it who construed his

Wally: I love this example. It's such a great example of determination and a picture of positive thinking. Evaluate your shot, plan it, then execute it.

Our goal, then, on any given round should be to give 100% on every shot and leave the results up to the swing and to the elements.

promenade as nothing more than a piece of showmanship, he returned, quickly chose his club and played the stroke.

The happy ending, of course, would be that he holed it. In fact, he just failed to do so, the ball pitching a few inches short of the hole and ending in a bunker at the back of the green. But the moral is there all right. He refused to play that vital shot until he had planned it in detail, caring nothing for the derision which might follow were his plan not wholly successful.

Most of us are not of the moral stature of Hagen, and faced with a similar predicament in the monthly bogey, we should not like to run the risk of the mild ridicule which would follow were we seen snooping about the green, examining it in detail with our ball on the fairway two hundred yards behind us. But who is to know it if we have a clear picture of the shot in our mind, sharpened even to the point of seeing it disappear into the hole? At any rate, we could seek comfort inside the clubhouse, knowing that although we failed, we knew what we had to do and how we proposed to do it.

Tom: This chapter, Making A Plan, is what separates great players from good players. Hogan, Snead, Nelson, Palmer, Nicklaus, Trevino, Watson...the list goes on, they all had complete mastery of the mental side of golf. Even more than technique, this is where the game is truly played–in the mind.

XIV
THE SHORT PITCH

Another pitch to the flag, this time by Henry Cotton: I think this photograph speaks for itself—the body perfectly poised—the shot firmly played with the hands bringing the clubhead through after the ball.

LIVE HANDS

V
JUSTIFICATION

When a humble amateur, and a weekend golfer at that, writes a book on the game it is reasonable to ask him to state his justification. He must explain his confounded cheek. My justification may be slender, but it is two-fold. Golf has formed a part of my life for the last thirty years, and to it I owe a very great deal. It is difficult to be connected with anything for so long without forming in that time certain fixed ideas.

I have admitted in an earlier chapter that when I had the time I studied the game and made experiments, and I am open to the accusations that I allocated more time to golf and less to other and more important things than I should have done in those days. But I do not regret it. It was fun. And if I partially neglected certain aspects of History, I think I learned something about golf. Besides, a modest connection with the game has given me opportunities to study at close quarters the methods of many of its best players, to discuss this elusive game with them, and even to play against some. So much for my first justification.

As I ploughed my crooked furrow through the tempting soil of theory, I was often conscious of the feeling of surfeit, of having too much of a good thing. Yet each field seemed more fertile than the last and I could not resist to plough through it. It might have continued like that and one might have died a ploughman. I realized at last that the only thing to do was to stand aside and review the entire cultivation. What field or what area produced the richest crop? For there would be found the soil that was most worthwhile.

I decided then, and I have seen no reason to change, that the basis of the game of golf was the alliance between the hands and the clubhead. The closer and the more sensitive the alliance of these two, the better the player. It is this alliance which enables the good golfer to produce the shot again and again with an almost monotonous precision. It accounts for his excellent ball control, that ability to string the shots together and to place them where he wishes them to go.

It is the temporary rift in this alliance which causes us to score our sevens and eights after playing a few preceding holes in or near par figures. It may explain the light and shade of a lawn tennis player I once knew, who in a qualifying round of a

---

Wally: So remember, follow the principles in this book to become alive to the clubhead for a lasting swing feeling that will carry you through.

Tom: To me, there is almost nothing more amazing in golf than to see a good player in their later years, having lost most of their flexibility and strength, make a swing and nail it cleanly, exactly as he had planned. Though the swing may not be pretty, the hand action gives them away. It's like riding a bike; you never forget how to do it, and it's magic. At that point I turn to my caddy and say, "This guy knows how to play golf."

XV

THE FINAL TOUCHES TO THE PLAN

George Duncan has made his plan and is adding the final touches to it before he plays the shot. See how the hands are feeling for the clubhead. Before he undertakes the shot, his hands will give the club a last flick, and then the vital spark will jump from the clubhead to the hands. Duncan is a great example of a player who makes his plan quickly and carries it through with the minimum delay.

tournament, went out in 54 and came home in 32!

However lighthearted a player might be, and golf was meant to be enjoyed, he is a liar if he denies that he wishes to play as well as his limitations will allow. Yet I believe it is a fact that nine out of every ten weekend golfers are not making the most of the golf that is in them.

I feel they are not doing so, because their game is not based on any sound formula, a formula known to the player to which he will turn when playing badly and on which he can then rebuild his game. Even with the best the game of golf turns in cycles. There is the crescendo to the peak of form. There is that glorious lightheaded and dizzy period when we reach and remain at the peak, so confident as a rule, that we think of nothing but hitting the ball and hitting it as hard as

Wally: There is a great swing in every golfer. The way to bring this swing out is by becoming alive to the hands and the alliance of the hands and the clubhead.

we can. According to our ability there follows either a crash or a gradual slither downward from the champagne heights of success. This is the time when our game should receive an overhaul, a time when we should return to first principles to see if they are being neglected. But first we must decide what these principles are. We must base our game on something.

Many handicap players express surprise when it is suggested to them that they are not completely dead-handed; that they are not swinging the clubhead with the hands; and that the only limbs in direct contact with the club are being left far behind in the mad rush with the body to get at the ball. Either completely baffled or obsessed with the importance of some movement in the swing and exaggerating its importance in consequence, they struggle on hoping that things will come right. A sound formula is lacking to help them regain their game.

I believe that by thinking only of his

hands, by swinging the club with them, and by hitting the ball with the hands, through the medium of the clubhead, the long handicap golfer can take strokes off his game. I believe this since I have seen it happen frequently. I have seen players in the course of a round find a golf swing they never possessed before. Their movements, previously stilted and labored, have suddenly become natural and have fitted smoothly into place. They did so, firstly, because the swing was properly controlled, and secondly, because these movements were not studied. The player's energy was redirected to the only object of the golf swing, namely to hit the ball. His game gained in control since he was swinging the clubhead with the hands, conscious of it throughout the swing, and bringing it to the ball with the only part of his anatomy capable of the task, that is to say, the hands. I believe, also, that if we are playing badly, attention to this formula will do more than anything to revive in us this feeling, the feeling of something to hit with, without which we cannot play golf.

The close relationship between the hands and the clubhead is not an innovation. The best swings have honored it since golf began. It has been recognized by the best players of recent years. But in playing with friends in the higher handicap grades, I formed the notion that it was not as widely recognized as it might have been.

There is an old proverb which says, "He that bewaileth himself hath the cure in his hands."

And that is my second justification.

XVI
THE HIGH PITCH

Sam Snead, the British Open Champion, at the finish of a high pitch. Here we have Control and Balance.

Why?

By this time I can safely leave the answer to you.

LIVE HANDS

For information on Wally Armstrong's golf clinics, schools, video tapes and books, write: Wally Armstrong, Gator Golf, P.O. Box 941911, Maitland, FL 32794.

For information on Wally Armstrong's Performance Pack, featuring Wally Armstrong's Golf Log, Audio Golf Tips and Golf Drill Cards, Call or write: Sports Log Publishers, P.O. Box 9275, South Laguna, CA 92677, (800) 327-6303.